W. E. Borah

The Closing Argument of W. E. Borah for the Prosecution in the Great Coeur d'Alene Riot-Murder Trial

W. E. Borah

The Closing Argument of W. E. Borah for the Prosecution in the Great Coeur d'Alene Riot-Murder Trial

ISBN/EAN: 9783337306588

Printed in Europe, USA, Canada, Australia, Japan

Cover: Foto ©Suzi / pixelio.de

More available books at **www.hansebooks.com**

THE CLOSING ARGUMENT OF W. E. BORAH
FOR THE PROSECUTION, IN THE GREAT
COEUR D'ALENE RIOT-MURDER TRIAL, DE-
LIVERED JULY 27, 1899, WALLACE, IDAHO.இ.இ

STATEMENT.

The trial of Paul Corcoran for the killing of James Cheyne, which took place at Wallace, Idaho, in July, 1899, grew out of the Coeur d'Alene mining riots of April 29, 1899. Upon the last named date, about one thousand men, a large portion of whom were armed and masked, congregated at Wardner and destroyed the Bunker Hill and Sullivan mine and killed two men, one by the name of Smith and one James Cheyne. Among others indicted for the murder of Cheyne, was Paul Corcoran, who was put upon trial at Wallace, Idaho, in July, 1899. The trial lasted some three weeks and was one of the most exciting murder trials that has taken place in the northwest. Hon. George H. Stewart, of Boise, Idaho, was called to preside. The prosecution was represented by J. H. Forney, of Moscow, Idaho, special prosecutor, assisted by Hon. J. H. Hawley and W. E. Borah, of Boise, Idaho. The defense was represented by Colonel Pat Reddy, of San Francisco; F. C. Robertson, of Spokane; Pat Breen, of Butte, and Jones & Morphy, of Wallace, Idaho. The jury returned a verdict of guilty of murder in the second degree.

The Closing Argument for the Prosecution of W. E. Borah, in the Great Coeur d' Alene Riot-Murder Trial, Delivered July 27, 1899, Wallace, Idaho.

May it please your Honor and Gentlemen of the Jury:

It now devolves upon me, as one of the counsel for the State, to close this argument, upon behalf of the State.

I desire to say in the beginning that I regret as much as any one that Colonel Reddy was compelled, on account of illness, to unexpectedly close his argument. His closing words, which intimated that he expected an attack from me, discloses the fact that he misunderstands his adversary. I have no contention whatever with Colonel Reddy with reference to his personal bearing or conduct in this case; there are matters of deeper concern than the personal conduct of counsel, and it is with such matters I wish exclusively to deal.

Much has been said by opposing counsel in this case with reference to myself. They seem to have selected me as the particular one upon whom to pour out their studied abuse, and against whom they should frantically hurl their long-nursed invective. It may be well to say, therefore, that I concede the defense the right at all times if they so choose to attack me, and if I am not able to take care of myself it will not necessarily result in an injury to any one except myself. Anything the attorneys have done upon the part of the defense toward me personally, I apprehend has been in a measure actuated by a desire to serve their client, even if in doing so they bordered upon unprofessional conduct, or wandered somewhat from the ethics of gentlemen. I realize that when men are defending a man for crime and putting forth every effort within their power for the purpose of releasing him, that it is their province and their privilege to adopt any course of procedure that they may choose to adopt, so long as they act within the law and within that code of morals which is ordinarily observed by members of my profession; and if they choose to be insensible to the higher impulses and principles of the profession I shall not linger to quarrel even then. I asked for no protection at the time they made the attack; I ask for none now. I can say, therefore, that I bid Colonel Reddy good-bye, with the best wishes for the restoration of health and for a long and prosperous future.

Gentlemen of the Jury, this case presents a strange condition of affairs. As has been suggested to you by other counsel, it presents a condition of affairs which never existed before in this State and under exactly similar circumstances nowhere else. We find that upon the 29th day of April, 1899, in the very midst of a civilized and an apparently well-ordered community, that a thousand or more men deliberately banded themselves together and went forth in the open light of day, evidently for the purpose of committing not only the crime of arson but of indiscriminate murder. That condition of affairs existed in the county in which you live, and in the State in which I live; that condition of affairs existed and exists under the system of laws which are the only shelter you and I can claim for our homes and our lives. The fact that men should have had the self-assurance and unhesitating belief that they could go forth in the open light of day, and in the very presence of the officers of the law, and in the very face of an onlooking community, and not only commit one crime but a multitude of crimes, not only kill one person but perhaps a dozen, is proof positive that there is something radically wrong in the conditions under which they have been permitted to bring that assurance unto themselves. It shows that back of this terrible crime is the hellish connivance of men sworn to execute the law—back of it is the arch-conspiracy to supplant your whole theory of government with the unbridled power of men given over to lawlessness and revenge.

Who should thwart their purpose? Who will be brave enough, and manly enough, and patriotic enough to give back law and order to this region of untold wealth and of magnificent beauty? The Commonwealth is making its last appeal to you. Should you falter there is no power beyond, to which we can apply. With the jury rests the grand possibility of ridding this region of these awful and soul-sickening crimes which for more than seven years have brought sorrow to good people and shame and chagrin to our entire State.

3

Gentlemen, much has been said in this case also with reference to unfairness upon the part of the prosecution, and many parties whom they fancy are connected with the prosecution have been attacked, and especially the State officers. Although Mr. Sinclair has nothing to do with this case, although Dr. France has scarcely been upon the witness stand, although the Governor has but engaged in the faithful discharge of his duties as Chief Executive of the State, although these officers have had nothing whatever to do with anything upon which you have to pass or sit in judgment, yet they have been persistently and viciously attacked. They have been viciously accused of all kinds of misconduct. In the very face of this attack, however, they admit that so weak and so powerless were the county authorities upon the 29th day of April, that men could go forth in the open and commit the crime of murder and never be embarrassed or checked in the act or arrested after the foul crime was known to every one. This attack simply shows, therefore, the cloven foot of the defense. It would seem that they would rather confine their efforts to disproving facts which show guilt upon the part of the defendant than to indiscriminate and puerile attacks upon the public officers who are seeking to enforce the law. But so despised, so hated and abhorred by these criminal combinations in this community are those who even respect the law, that it stirs all the venom of their being to have the respresentatives of law anywhere around.

CORONER'S JURY.

It has been said also that the defendant has not been given a fair trial, for the reason that he has been deprived of looking into the investigation which has been made upon the part of the Coroner when engaged in the work of ferreting out the parties responsible for this crime. This murder of which the defendant stands charged was not committed by the defendant alone. He is not the only party against whom the State will be compelled to proceed. Many others are charged with this killing, some of whom are at large and fugitives from justice today. Now, shall the State be charged with unfairness simply because it refuses to divulge the names of those fugitives, as it would do, should it expose the Coroner's evidence? The State has some rights, and this is one of them, and it is given to the State by the statute.

This Coroner's investigation is one provided for by our statutes, and the statutes also prescribe the manner in which it shall be conducted. They have not shown you, nor neither can they, that Coroner France has violated the statutes or the law with reference to Coroner's proceedings; they have not shown you or the Court that the law in this regard has gone unobserved in the least, but simply because the Coroner saw fit to close the doors of this investigation, as by law he had a right to do, they would have you believe the defendant has been deprived of some right. Dr. France was engaged in the difficult task of tearing the masks off the men who wore them upon the 29th day of April, and because he has performed this task fearlessly and without faltering, he is denounced as unfair. But all men are unfair, and are traitors to these defendants, who would uncover the dastardly participants of that most brutal and unexcusable of crimes of the 29th. Dr. France was a sworn officer; he had his duty to perform; the law prescribed his course, and without hesitation he followed the behests of a good citizen. He could not do, for he was too good a citizen, as certain other officers did, encourage this affair or seek to conceal its participants; he could not trail along like a conscious and self-confessed recreant of duty in the tracks of crime. It was the same question with him that is now presented to you—Which is the stronger, the arm of crime or the arm of the law? That is the question he had to determine and it is the question you will have to determine by your verdict. I admit that he acted rigidly and with great determination, but great crimes like these necessarily demand strong and determined action.

NO ATTACK UPON LABOR UNIONS.

Much has been said here, also, to the effect that we are making an attack upon labor unions, and that we have denounced these organizations as criminal organizations in their inception. I think the counsel have misunderstood us, or at least they would like to have you misunderstand us. I am not inclined to believe that counsel are so much misled as that they would like to have you misled upon this particular proposition.

Counsel know full well that no one representing or connected with this prosecution has ever said that these organizations were criminal organizations in thier inception; that union labor organizations, as such, are either objectionable or criminal. The only thing I have said and the only thing for which we contend here, is that at a certain time, a time which we have shown you in this case, these organizations became criminal organizations; that they transferred their efforts from the honest and high-minded efforts which they might have put forth as they were originally organized, into an effort to assault, drive out, kill and murder those who did not care to become members of the organization.

Gentlemen, men have a perfect right to organize, to combine their efforts, and as I shall attempt to show you later, they not only have the right, but in my judgment it is their duty so to do. It is a laudable and noble thing to do. They not only have the right to organize, but they have the right to induce, by moral suasion, or any other reasonable mode known to man, to have outsiders join their organization and to become active members thereof. A union man has a perfect right to go into the different places in this camp and ask that the non-union men join the union organizations; they have a perfect right to have their deputies over the camp for the purpose of enlarging their membership.

But they have no right, and here is the parting of the ways—they have no right simply because a man does not join the union to go forth, behind masks and armed cap-a-pie, assault, beat, shoot down—shoot him as he runs for his life as they did James Cheyne. Does any true friend of labor, any honest union man claim such a right? And yet this, as I shall show you, the members of the Miners' Union of the Cœur d'Alenes did upon the 29th of April last. Thus we condemn the labor organizations here upon trial, for that, and for nothing more. Had they remained in the canyon, had they remained at their labors, had these organizations kept where evidently they were in the first instance to be kept—within the legitimate duties and powers of such organizations, no one would find fault with them; rather would they have received the kindly support of all good citizens, for labor organizations within this scope, given them by their true leaders are to be encouraged and protected.

What the State claims here is that about the 22d day of April, and perhaps for some time prior and on and up until the 29th, these local labor organizations in the Cœur d'Alenes took upon themselves to commit crime, to drive

out the employees of the Bunker Hill and Sullivan Mining
Company, to destroy the property of the company, to burn
homes and to take lives of innocent men, and that when
they undertook to do this they then became criminal organizations. If the members of a church should meet as
such around the altar of worship today to formulate a plan
to rob a bank tomorrow, the sanctity of the organization
would not shield them. No one claims that these organizations are, in and of themselves, criminal organizations,
but the claim is that they became such by undertaking to
do that which the laws of the State forbid and which your
consciences forbid also. "By their acts, ye shall judge
them."

At the same time, we would not want you to understand
for a moment that we are asking for any vicarious atone-
ment here. We do not want Mr. Corcoran, nor any one
else, convicted unless we have met in full measure the high
standard of proof required by law. We do not want to
use the conviction of an innocent man to deter others in
the commission of crime; it is not our desire to have any
one punished simply that we may hold up the verdict to
the community and say if any one even attempts such
crimes they can and will be punished.

But we do desire that in case you find that the defendant
was connected with this conspiracy, in case you find that
his relation to the conspiracy was such as to make him responsible under the instructions of the Court, in case you
find that he gave voice or encouragement to the awful
crime, or, like Saul of old, was consenting thereto, that you
fearlessly and without faltering, do your duty. Do not
permit the fact that some unpleasant consequences may
result from the verdict deter you in doing your full duty.
The golden-haired, bright-eyed little girl, nestling in her
father's arms, the little family, seemingly crouching under
the impending fate, awaken in my heart, and I know they
must in yours, emotions hard to control. But you, as citizens, cannot do that which the father, upon the 29th of
April, refused to do. When he placed that mask over his
face and hid the face of crime from the eyes of the world,
he also changed the face of a father to that of an outlaw.
It would seem that if there was no man in the Cœur d'Alenes
brave enough to tear the mask from his face, as there was
not, still the memory of those little ones, whom he now
hugs to his bosom, ought to have made him brave enough

to do it himself. But in that hour, his family ceased to be a shield. After that, good citizens will not be disturbed by the appeals of counsel. It is simply the old story—ten thousand times, mother, or sister or daughter has stood by the prison bars, frozen into a statue of grief, and yet in order that society may be protected, that we may have a government under which families can be reared and homes maintained, jurors must be brave enough and manly enough to do their duty.

NO QUESTION OF WAGES.

There is another feature of this case that I want you to think about. Men inevitably sympathize with the man who toils, and especialy do they sympathize with him in these open conflicts between labor and capital, too often brought on by the grasping greed of avarice. Especially is this true where the laborer is being cut down in wages— when he sees his loved ones deprived of the necessaries of life. But upon the 29th day of April there were no differences whatever between the Bunker Hill and Sullivan Mining Company and the union or between the company and its employees, with reference to wages. Nothing of that kind in any shape or form. Those matters had all been settled. The wages had been raised, and upon April 29th every man in the employ of the company was willing to go to work if the union men would permit them to do so. But upon the same day that perfect peace rested upon the works of the Bunker Hill and Sullivan Company, so far as the company and its employees were concerned, these union men gathered themselves together some twenty miles away, took their rifles, their dynamite and their masks and went there and destroyed the mill, burned homes, ransacked and robbed dwellings and killed two men. What was it that actuated those men? It was hatred, revenge— despicable, cowardly revenge. They were enraged, not because wages had been cut, but because the company refused to accede to their demands and discharge their old non-union employees. Are there any mitigating circumstances surrounding the crime committed under such conditions? Had any one been deprived of work, oppressed in any way? Had wages been lowered? No; they had been raised. These men were actuated by the spirit of hatred alone. Furthermore, looking back over the last seven years of lawlessness in this canyon, cognizant of the connivance of the Sheriff—miserable tool of theirs—they had the assurance that they could do all these things, and, as the defendant said, "return at night and go to work," unmolested. The last seven years of this particular portion of Shoshone County made them bold. They have grown stronger and bolder as the years passed, and they propose to rule regardless of the laws of the State. But in this instance the outraged conscience of a whole Commonwealth demanded that something be done, and while they were not followed back by any Sheriff, they were pursued by the condemnation of the whole State. Close behind them stalked retribution with uplifted spear.

UNDISPUTED FACTS.

There are a great many things in this case that are practically admitted; there are many things that the defense has not in any way undertaken to meet, and I desire to call your attention to those particular matters before going into what may be called the controverted questions. First, of course, it is admitted, as has been said, that a terrible crime was committed upon the 29th of April. Perhaps you will never listen again to a narrative so revolting as that of Mr. Pipes and Mrs. Sinclair, with reference to the murder of James Cheyne; the facts as narrated by Mr. Pipes, leading up to the murder, and the facts as given by Mrs. Sinclair, as having transpired during the killing Thus, we say, the crime is admitted. There is no contention with reference to that, so we may pass it for the time being, although it may perhaps be necessary to refer to it in another way hereafter. Second, it is practically admitted that whoever committed this crime was actuated solely by revenge. Mr. Cheyne was in the peaceable pursuit of an honest livelihood, and the only brand that was upon him was that of non-unionism. My eloquent friend from Spokane told you upon yesterday, in speaking of the motive for the murder, that there was a question of wages here which was calculated to irritate men, calculated to arouse men's passions, and I thought before he closed he was going to justify the killing of Cheyne upon the ground of the insufficiency of wages. I was unable to comprehend his logic except upon that theory. He referred you to the Homestead strike; he referred you to the fact that the Bunker Hill and Sullivan paid seventy thousand dollars ($70,000) less wages than that which, in the counsel's judgment, they ought to pay. Seeking to come at the facts therefore, as they existed upon the 29th of April, let us see whether there were any differences there upon that day with reference to the question of wages. Was there any employee in the company's employment upon that day who was demanding higher wages? Was there any one who had any right to speak upon this subject or who was in any way affected by the wages, complaining? Were the employees irritated? Where were the employees of the Bunker Hill and Sullivan at the time the train left Burke and Gem? They were starting to their work; they were going about their business; they were satisfied with their employment and their wages; there were no disturbances. It was quite unlike the Homestead strike, where there was a reduction of wages and men were thrown out of employment and thrown out of home. These men were in the emply and could continue in the employ of the company, and any one could have entered their employ if they had been willing to go in there with the non-union men, but that was the bone of contention. It was not the question of wages, but the question of unionism or non-unionism. They refused, in other words, to be satisfied with a settlement of the wage question, but these men upon the train had another demand and that was the recognition of the union; the displacement of the man who had his home and his little family; the driving out of the camp the man who had been at work for the company for five or six years, had accumulated some means upon which to live; they said, "You must recognize the union," and as they explained to you, that means the employment of union men and union men alone. There was no wage question between them; there were no differences of that kind; it was simply the determination on the part of these unions to absolutely control that mine the same as they control the others, even if it was necessary to take human life in order to do so.

That brings us, gentlemen, to that which we are always anxious to find with reference to a crime, and that is the motive. That is, the actuating and impelling power, and upon whom did it operate? Who but the Miners' Unions of the Cœur d'Alenes had any cause to quarrel with the Bunker Hill and Sullivan Mining Company? Who wished to change their regulations? Who felt aggrieved at them because they refused to change their regulations? Nobody except the men who had joined these organizations, the organizations which had made up their minds that they would control the situation. Who but union men would denounce Cheyne as a "scab" and justify his killing because he was a "scab," as the evidence shows in this case the fiendish devils did, who stood above him as he lay there in the gutter writhing in the agony of death? We find here, therefore, the motive, the actuating and impelling power, that which caused those men to congregate upon the morning of the 29th, take possession of the train, go there with arms and dynamite for the purpose of destroying the company's property and of driving out the non-union men. Who had any malice against this company except the union? Who had any motive for running Cheyne out of the country except the union which he refused to join? Who had any reason to denounce him as a "scab," except those who look upon "scabs" as outlaws? Why was that bullet fired with deadly aim into his vitals—it was no stray shot—no one but those members of the union who apparently believe that because a man is a non-union man that they have a right, under the laws of this State, to kill with impunity Therefore, we find, in the very inception, a motive for this crime, a reason for it; we find the power which brought them together and took them to Wardner. We find the feeling and force around which this conspiracy was organized from the 13th day of April until the 29th.

We might say, therefore, gentlemen of the jury, that not only is it clearly proven and practically undisputed that this crime was actuated by a feeling of revenge, but it is also proven and undisputed that it was committed by the members of the Cœur d'Alene Miners' Union. Understand me when I say that it is practically admitted, because it is in no sense denied, when they had it in their power to deny it. We have shown you that from the 23d until the 29th, Ed. Boyle, the President of the Wardner Union, was at the head of his mob, constantly agitating upon the streets of Wardner, inciting men to riot and to crime; not only obtruding himself upon the company and its employees, but going into private houses, firing through the windows or through the doors, driving out "scabs," as he called them, driving them down the hill. Who was it that was doing this? It was Ed. Boyle. It has been brought home to him. Where is Ed. Boyle in this case? If those things are not true, what has become of this gentleman? Loyal as he must be to the union, why does he not remove this stigma from the Wardner Miners' Union? Why does he not relieve the supersensitive soul of counsel who go into a frenzy when we mention the Miners' Union? If he lied when he made that speech about the 27th, in which he said the unions of the Cœur d'Alenes were back of him, why does not some officer of the union seek to be heard?

Mr. Robertson complained in his argument that we have produced in this connection a wonderful identifier, a man with a marvelous eye, an eagle eye, and he proceeds to find great fault with him because upon the occasion of Mr. Boyle's leading his mob through the boarding house, he testified that within two or three minutes he saw thirty-eight men in a crowd of one hundred and fifty whom he knew. The names of those men were given here. Mr. Edward Boyle, the leader of the crowd, was signaled out and named. The other names were given and the parties described. Now, if this witness was mistaken in the men whom he identified, or the number whom he identified; if perchance he overlooked a man or got a man too many, or if he was lying absolutely, it was easily within the power of the defense to prove all these things. But no one of these men identified comes forward to say they were not there. Mr. Boyle himself is silent, and the only witness who has testified against our witness was the counsel in his argument. Mr. Boyle is not called; the men whose names were given are not called to testify that they were not there; no member of the Wardner Union who has been charged as being a co-conspirator has dared to open his lips before this jury to remove the charge brought directly home to the Wardner Union.

Again counsel complains that Mr. Burbidge stated to you that the union was in charge of their tramway upon the 26th. We claim to have shown that certain members of the union did have charge of this tramway. It may be that our witnesses were mistaken, but are you not willing to believe them so long as they stand unimpeached or un-contradicted, and so long as those other men whose names have been called out are within call of the court house and dare not come here to tell you that Mr. Burbidge stated a falsehood or that they were not in fact in charge of this tramway? There are times, gentlemen of the jury, when silence is itself a confession of crime, and I say to you that instead of talking loud and long here for the benefit of the public, to the effect that the Miners' Unions are innocent of this crime, it would be better, so long as they have the calling power, to bring the President and the officers and

12

the men whose names have been called to disprove this charge that has been brought against them. It was within their power to do it; they are in touch with the union; the counsel for the defense are counsel for the union, as they say, and yet no man has raised his voice in defense of the union except counsel by way of argument.

I remember another thing that my friend Robertson stated when he opend this case on the part of the defense. He told you he would introduce the by-laws and the constitutions—the creed of these men, that you might see it and observe it. We tried to introduce them but you observe that we could not sufficiently identify them. We had printed by-laws and constitutions and yet were confronted with the extraordinary condition of affairs that the ex-President of the union had never seen its constitution and by-laws. They knew nothing about them whatever. But while they refused to permit us to introduce them, they pledged you in the opening of this case that they would introduce them, but they are not here. When we ask where they are, the echo answers, "Where!" Can it be possible that this organization, which has its constitution and by-laws, has become so debased in its purposes and its workings by the men who have taken charge of it that they dare not expose to this jury the rules and regulations? We can only say that they are not here. You are deprived of the privilege of looking into them. They have withheld this evidence which is within their possession.

The defense insists also that we have not shown that the subordinates acted in obedience to their superiors, as the prosecuting attorney said we would do when he opened the case. You remember Mr. Eri appeared upon the witness stand and he was an ex-President—next to an ex-President of the United States, apparently, from the manner in which he spoke—but when that man came to him at the mouth of the tunnel and told him to do certain things upon the morning of the 29th, did he hesitate; did he ask any questions; did he refuse in any manner to act? Suppose a masked man should come to you and say to you: "I want you to take a mask and go to a certain point and wait for other parties," the first thing you would say would be: "Who are you?" But Eri did not say who are you, or why should you do this, but he went immediately; he obeyed like the cringing slave of a Sultan.

Then we have Mr. Lenecke, who received instructions

from some one and he goes down to Kellogg—follows the instructions to the letter. What else does he do? Takes along a pair of overalls, and you heard what he said with reference to them. He knew why he was taking those overalls. He knew he was taking them for the purpose of disidentifying himself—changing his clothes after he got upon the scene of action so that the people who saw him walk through the streets could not identify him by the clothes he had on. Yet so implicitly did he obey the man of authority that he took his clothes and mask according to instructions, and when he got upon the witness stand he had the temerity to say to you "He thought it was going to rain." Took them to keep the rain off his new pants. My opinion is when he testified to that, he was obeying his superior again.

Then we have this man Anderson, up the canyon. Two men appear from out the mouth of that tunnel, as he says, with cigars in their mouths and well dressed. Now notice the training which this man had received, because all this relates to the question of this conspiracy, as we will show you later. Two men appear at the mouth of the tunnel; he says he did not know them, but they gave him certain instructions, told him to do certain things, and it turned out that he obeyed them so implicitly that we find him down there on the day of the commission of the crime, twenty miles away from his work. Now, I ask you, gentlemen, in all candor, what was the influence, what was the power, from whence came the training that enabled officers and men to go to the mouths of tunnels and drive every single man out of employment in thirty minutes; put them upon a train and ship them twenty miles away with rifles on their backs and masks on their faces? Do you think that there has been no training; do you think that there is no organization here; is there no master whom these men follow; did they all get into Wardner by accident; did they drop out of the sky, or did they go there by reason of the fact that they had been so instructed, so ordered by their superiors, whose instructions and orders they obeyed implicitly? How conclusively this proves the organization, the understanding within the organization, and obedience to the officers, you alone must determine

Gentlemen of the jury, there is another fact with reference to the undisputed questions in this case, because it is another proposition left undenied when it was within the power of the defense to deny and disprove it if the same is untrue. They have not seen fit to go into the question of rebutting the proof introduced upon the part of the State to the effect that the union labor organizations formed a conspiracy to destroy this property and drive out the employees of the company. Notwithstanding the State has proven here that certain parties gave these orders, that the members followed certain instructions, notwithstanding we have brought this matter directly home to Mr. Boyle, Mr. Deevy and other officers of the organization, they have not seen fit to come here before this jury and deny any of these matters. Am I not justified, then, in saying to this jury, notwithstanding the bitter attack of counsel for the defense, notwithstanding they say that the union labor organizations had nothing to do with the matter, I say is it not fair for me to say to you that you are entitled to believe the State's evidence and to act upon it so long as they have not seen fit to deny these statements or rebut such proofs when it was within their power to do so if the State is either mistaken or has given you false testimony? If the defense were in a position where they could not bring forth this evidence it would be different; but they are standing here with the labor organizations behind them making a fight, as their counsel says, in defense not only of the defendant, but of these labor organizations, with all the Presidents and Vice-Presidents and Secretaries who are not fugitives from justice in close consultation with the defense—yet not one of them dare go upon the stand and dispute these facts.

PROOF OF CONSPIRACY.

Counsel for the defense have argued ably to the effect that no conspiracy has been proven. I want to say a word in reference to that, although my associate, Mr. Hawley, has covered that subject very completely. Permit me, however, to refresh your recollection in regard to one or two matters touching the subject of the proof of the conspiracy.

In the first place, I have reviewed the action at Wardner somewhat and it is fresh in your mind, and we need not go over that again, but let us see as to the action of organizations at other towns. You will remember that there was a lady from Mullen upon the witness stand who testified that upon the morning of the 29th there was a gathering in the town of from one hundred and fifty to two hundred men. That they gathered in front of the Miners' Union hall, and seemed well organized; men walked up and down the line, gave orders, and with military precision these men marched away from the Miners' Union hall on their way, as they cried out, "On to Wardner." This witness was a school teacher, wholly disinterested and wholly reliable. Immediately after her testimony, comes the testimony of Joe Riddell. Counsel for the defense seemed to like Joe, and they don't like him any better than I do, because his evidence here shows every single element that it is necessary to show in order to prove a conspiracy. His evidence not only shows that the Miners' Union of Mullen were acting in this matter under instruction and in concert with the other unions from the other towns, but it also shows that from the time they left the hall they had in their mind a criminal purpose which actuated them in their going. I want you jurymen to bear in mind the fact that this criminal purpose was not engendered after they reached the scene of the murder, after they had gotten upon the ground, but that it is a part and parcel of their thoughts, their mental make-up from the very time that they marched out of these towns under marching orders until they arrived at the place of the killing. They might have blown up the mill with dynamite alone, but, according to Joe Riddell's testimony, the first thing that the Mullen Union got hold of, and it is apparent they knew just where they were, were rifles. He says they went over to an old barn and dug them out of some refuse; dug out two or three boxes of rifles. It is not necessary for the State to show who hid those rifles there, but when you see one hundred and fifty or two hundred men marching out under marching orders and directly to the point where the rifles are buried, stop, gather them up, then you have conclusive proof that there was in their minds a previous knowledge of where to find them and a well determined purpose already formed in execution of which they were to be taken. They did not need any rifles merely to blow up the mill—they could do that with dynamite—but they did need rifles for the purpose of committing that other crime for which this defendant is being tried; it was, beyond question, a part and parcel of the conspiracy—that is, to drive out the employees, and, if necessary in doing so, to kill and murder. Now, do you think at the time those men left Mullen, one hundred and fifty or two hundred strong, under marching orders, that there was no organization behind them? Do you think that no one had seen them prior to this gathering and arranged for the gathering and the marching? Do you think no one had informed them why they should meet, where they should go, how they should go, why they should arm and where they should get arms? Men do not congregate together and start out upon such a march by accident; it all shows a design; it shows organization; it shows a well arranged purpose; and the only people who could formulate that design, arrange that organization and create that purpose for these movements were the superiors, the officers of this organization, the financial secretaries, such as this defendant.

Next we go to the town of Gem and we have the same thing there; the same prior knowledge of what they are to do; the same complete understanding of where they are to gather. We find them going down to the union hall and there you see guns stacked by the side of the sanctuary, the sanctuary where the laborer takes an oath to guard and protect the interest of his co-laborers. We find all the miners there from the mines; everything is in preparation; masks have been made, the guns have been arranged for, and when they go into the hall, so precise was the arrangement that the window blinds were closed and there in the darkness, hidden from the light of day, they take up their guns and put on their masks. What does all this disclose? A criminal purpose upon the part of the members of this organization, which was many miles away from the Mullen organization, but which was moving at the same time apparently under the same orders, with the same military precision toward the same point and apparently with the same ultimate design. Did all this happen by accident? Was there no organization, no plan, no understanding?

But counsel say these men were going upon a peaceful errand to give "moral support to the Wardner union." What an insult to your intelligence! Why this dynamite? Why these rifles? Why conceal themselves behind masks? Why darken their meeting places? It was the instinct of crime; fear already possessed their craven, cowardly souls. Conscience! Conscience!—the implacable and smiting spirit of justice had made cowards of them all. For "Man, wretched man, whenever he stoops to sin, feels with the act strong remorse within."

At almost the same hour that they were moving thus, at Gem, we find that they are gathering at the Miners' Union hall in the town of Burke. Over one hundred and fifty or two hundred men came together, and as we shall see in a few moments, the man who was at the head of that movement, the man who controlled that end of the conspiracy, was the defendant in this case. We find them doing at Burke just as they did at Gem and Mullen and the other towns, congregating around the Miners' Union hall and taking up their march to the train. The leader at Mullen had his duties to perform; the leader at Gem had his duties to perform; the leader at Burke had his portion of the conspiracy to look after; the Wardner Union had made arrangements to meet them, and now, as we shall show you pretty soon, this very defendant was one of the men who was in supreme control of this conspiracy, forming, guiding and directing it.

We ask you, therefore, Was there a conspiracy? Not that these men got together and deliberately entered into a partnership, as counsel for the defense say they must have done, or signed an agreement to do a certain thing. The Court will instruct you that it is not necessary that there be any agreement between them; it is only necessary that they act with a common design and for a common purpose and with a common and ultimate object in view. In this case, we find these men and the unions, although many miles apart, almost at the same hour of the day, acting apparently with the same purpose in view, with the same design, making the same preparations, moving in the same direction and arriving finally at the same destination. How did it happen? Was it by accident or design? No, no, you must be satisfied that it was all understood. That between the members of these unions and especially the officers there was a positive understanding that upon the 29th day of April every union should gather its men together, provide them with arms and masks and send them forth for the purpose of destroying the Bunker Hill and Sullivan mill and to drive out the non-union employees. They all arrived at the same point by the same train, at the same time, and when they got there, from that moment, they became,

18

in the eye of the law, one individual, the act of one was the
act of all. I ask you to bear in mind the startling fact that
there was scarcely a hitch in this movement from the time
it began until they returned after the crime had been committed upon the night of the 29th.

WHAT IS A CONSPIRACY.

Gentlemen of the jury, what is a conspiracy? Colonel
Reddy has said it is a comprehensive thing. So it is, and
about as comprehensive a conspiracy as has happened in
this portion of the country was this same conspiracy of the
29th of April. I have called your attention to the fact
that in my judgment you will be instructed that no actual
agreement, in the sense in which we ordinarily understand
the word, is necessary to constitute a conspiracy; it was
only necessary that we find them acting together, apparently with a common design and for a common purpose,
and if you so find that is sufficient to constitute a conspiracy.

Counsel for the defense has said, with a great deal of
candor, although I am not quite satisfied that he appre-
ciated the effect of it when he said it, that if we show in
this case that the defendant was a member of this conspiracy and that Cheyne was killed as a result of the conspiracy, that the State has established its case. I am going
to accept that proposition, not only as the law coming from
the defense as they interpret it, but for the reason that I
believe that it will prove to be the law from a higher source,
and that is from the Court. In other words, the act of one
is the act of all after the conspiracy is formed. Colonel
Reddy has said that we have abandoned the idea that this
man fired the shot or held the gun that killed Mr. Cheyne.
While that is a pretty broad proposition to state, and although we have proven it so closely that it would be no
violent presumption to infer the fact, yet the Court will
undoubtedly instruct you that after a conspiracy is formed,
after they have entered upon their unlawful purpose, that
then the act of one man is the act of all, and it is immate-
rial who held the gun or fired the shot. In other words, if
you and I join together for the doing of an unlawful thing,
the fact that you may remain ten miles away while I go
and commit the crime does not relieve you either legally or
morally or exempt you from punishment. It might just as
well be said that when the James gang used to surround a
town for the purpose of robbing a bank that the man who

sat on a hill and guarded the gateways to the town while the men went down and shot the cashier and robbed the bank would be innocent while those in the bank were guilty of murder. When men band themselves together and go upon an unlawful purpose, make up their minds to violate law, from that time what one man who is a member of the combination does binds all. If we show, therefore, as Mr. Robertson said, that the defendant was a member of this conspiracy, that he was aiding, encouraging and abetting the doing of these unlawful things, we shall certainly be entitled to ask at your hands a verdict of conviciton. For if he aided or abetted or sent the mob fairly upon their errand, it would make no difference that the defendant remained in the town of Burke, and, as the defense has insisted, played hide-and-seek all day with the nanny goat and Maggie Murphy.

As I have said to you, it is not necessary that the defendant be upon the ground, although later I shall undertake to show by the evidence that he was in fact actually present and participated in the killing. I am now simply calling your attention to some general principles of law which govern in this case and which would hold them responsible, although you might conclude he was not personally present at the time the deceased was shot. In other words, if upon the morning of the 29th of April, Mr. Corcoran, the defendant, called his men together and organized them for the purpose of going to Wardner, to violate law, to destroy property and drive out the non-union employees—the fact that he himself remained behind while his army went forth to do the work, would not render him guiltless. He is responsible for the agencies which he employed, for the forces he put in motion. It makes no difference whether it is Mrs. Bodtkin sending a box of poisoned candy to her lover's wife or whether it is the defendant sending a man down the railroad track seventeen miles with a Winchester; the agency is there, the influence, the encouragement, the advice, and the responsibility is the same as though the principal were upon the ground. I desire you to remember this rule particularly, as we shall apply it more specifically when we come to discuss the question of the alibi.

Neither is it necessary for us to show that when the parties left Burke they especially or particularly had in mind the killing of Cheyne or the killing of any other person in particular. When a conspiracy is once proven to have been formed for an unlawful purpose, it is not necessary to show that a particular crime was in view. In other words, if the members of this conspiracy went to Wardner for the purpose of driving out the employees of the company, to intimidate, abuse, insult, assault them, and, if necessary, in order to accomplish their purposes, to injure or kill some one, and as a result of all this Cheyne was killed, each member of the conspiracy would be guilty of murder, although no one might have known, when they started upon their expedition of crime, that such a man as Cheyne was living. It would make no difference whether they really contemplated actual murder or not when they started; if they had in their minds the commission of unlawful acts which 'would have a tendency to take human life, then, in that event, each and every man connected with the conspiracy would be guilty of the crime of murder, if, from the act of any one of the conspirators, death was inflicted upon any one. The simple question is, did their unlawful acts have a tendency to cause death to any person? If so, any man who joined that conspiracy is responsible for the result of the tendency, and this is the responsibility which we would, in the first instance, fasten upon the prisoner at the bar.

We do not contend, of course, that Mr. Corcoran went to Wardner for the purpose of shooting the particular man who was shot; but we contend that he went there for an unlawful purpose, for the purpose of committing unlawful acts, and the result of the unlawful acts was the death of James Cheyne. If Corcoran was a member of that conspiracy, whether he held the gun or not, whether he was upon the ground or not, whether he knew of such a man as Cheyne or not, or whether he intended to murder any one in particular or not, he is guilty, for whatever any individual member of the conspiracy did in carrying out the general purposes, binds all, and for which each and all are responsible and must answer unto the law. The only question, therefore, as I was saying to you, is this, Was the defendant a member of that conspiracy? There is certainly no question about the existence of the conspiracy; it seems to me that that is a settled question. There is no question about this body of men arriving at the town of Wardner; there is certainly no question but that they went there for an unlawful purpose; there is certainly no question about the fact that Cheyne was killed by some one of this armed mob of men who went down upon the train; if, therefore, we find that the defendant in this case was a member of that conspiracy, we shall have established the case upon the part of the State. Later we shall go farther and try to show you that he was not only a member of the conspiracy but that he was there on the ground actually engaged in carrying out these overt acts which resulted in murder

A MEMBER OF THE CONSPIRACY.

In the first place, gentlemen of the jury, it is a settled fact in this case, that the defendant is the Financial Secretary of the Burke Union. Understand me, there is no contention on the part of the State that the mere fact of his being financial secretary makes him a conspirator. But we do claim that it is a most potent fact in the chain of evidence which goes to establish that he was a member of the conspiracy. Why? For the simple reason that it placed him in such a position, having charge of the office and familiar with its duties, that he must have had knowledge of the conspiracy which was undoubtedly organized by this very union at Burke. The things necessary to be done and which were done, could not go on without his knowledge, yea, more, without his consent. The organizing, the meeting of the men, the preparing arms, buying ammunition, preparing masks, these things would necessarily be brought home to him, and, furthermore, would require his approval. You know that the rank and file of these organizations did not organize this conspiracy; you know that the men who were down in the mines and working from day to day, the honest laborers and not the agitators, the masses as you may say, did not plan, organize and send forth this gigantic conspiracy. It was too perfect, it showed too much of design, it took too much time and preparation—the men who work every day are the men who think more of their homes and children and less of arson and murder. Besides, they had not the power to do so, they could not compel any one to obey them if they designed to do so. So we find, in the first instance, that this defendant is placed in a position where he must have known precisely what was going on. Yes, more. I contend from all the facts and circumstances proven in this case that the Burke Union would never have taken this step, would never have done as it did without the consent of its superior officer, and not only that, without his advice and encouragement

It is unreasonable to presume or suppose that those men would have come out of the mines, quit their work and gone upon this perilous expedition without not only the consent but the encouragement, advice and guidance of the man who stood as their superior, their leader. Consider for a moment the relation of these parties to this conspiracy and to these acts of April 29th. Here were the men working down in the mines, they were continuously engaged from day to day, satisfied with their wages, no strike pending; while upon the other hand, here was the defendant, the paid officer of that union, whose sole business was to acquaint himself with the affairs of the union, its details and its general affairs—the man in sole charge. He was in a position to acquaint himself with the mind of every single member of the organization at Burke, was he not? These things must have been brought to his knowledge in the very inception of the difficulty, for not only was he Secretary of the Union at Burke, but he was even nearer to the sole source of pewer—he was a member of what is called the Central Union.

We have shown in this case that there is in these organizations, what is called a Central Union, which seems to be the ne plus ultra of all power, excepting possibly the President of the Western Federation of Miners. It is a kind of concentrated power, regulating the affairs of all the different unions. From thence comes, as we claim, all power with reference to these organizations. The defendant, as has been shown, is a delegate to the Central Union and he stands at the very source of power with reference to all actions which can be had upon the part of subordinate unions. If it is true, as counsel for the defense insist, that the Central Union has nothing to do with such things; if it is true that the Central Union never acted upon this matter; if it is true that the Central Union never had anything to do with this question of the trouble between the Bunker Hill & Sullivan and the union men, am I not privileged to say to you, in all fairness, that the defense had it within their power to prove to you, in one hour's time, all these facts?

MR. ROBERTSON: I desire to challenge that line of argument on the ground it was the duty of the State to produce that in the first instance.

THE COURT: Very well, proceed with the argument.

MR. BORAH, continuing: As I was saying to you when interrupted by the gentleman from Spokane, this man stands at the very source of power. We have proven that he was a member of that union; we have proven that he was a member of the Central Union; we have proven that he was Financial Secretary of the Burke Union. We have also shown beyond all question that these organizations of which he was a member were the organizations, the members of which committed this crime. Whose duty was it, after such proof was made, after the crime was brought home to the union of which the defendant is a member and a controlling spirit, after we have shown that he stood at the source of power of these organizations which committed the crime, whose duty was it, I say, to remove that cloud and that stigma so sufficiently fastened in the first instance?

But, Colonel Reddy says that the defendant quit, that he retired from the conspiracy, that he ran away. from the tragedy before the commission of the crime. That would have been a magnificent defense, it would have been a complete and a sufficient defense in this case, because a conspirator may give notice to his co-conspirators that he absolves himself from all allegiance to the conspiracy and retires from the affair and thus exonerates himself for the wrongs which follow. But just as they have remained silent upon the question of the organization at Wardner, just as they have remained silent upon the power and position of the Central Union and the constitution and by-laws of the several unions, so they have remained silent upon this subject as to the time when the defendant changed his mind and when he broke away from the conspiracy. This matter, as the others, is left to be presented alone, without the support of evidence, by the eloquence of counsel.

We say, in all fairness, that we have brought these matters home to the defendant sufficently clear to satisfy a fair mind until they are met at least by rebutting evidence. Does the defendant stand at the source of power, was he connected with the organization by means of which the crime was perpetrated? If he was a leader, if he was in the place of power in the organigation, and if he was there upon the morning of the 29th of April, then when was it that the defendant broke away from the one hundred and fifty or two hundred men that left Burke under his inspiration to go to Wardner? The evidence of Mr. Culbertson shows that not only was the defendant connected with the organization officially, but he was actually present participating upon that morning—that the men were acting under his inspiration. When was it, therefore, that he made up his mind that he would rather transact a heavy day's business at Burke than go to Wardner? Mr. Reddy says this is precisely what he did do. That he changed his mind and remained at Burke; in other words, after he had organized this portion of the conspiracy and gathered his men together upon the 29th of April, after he had been there in their midst during the busy hour of preparation in the morning, he made up his mind he would go no farther

Let us analyze that position for a few moments and see, even if it is true, where it places the defendant. Let us take the position that the Colonel took in this matter and see where it places the defendant. That he made up his mind that he would not go to Wardner with the men with whom he had been in touch that morning, the men whom he had gathered together, as we claim the evidence shows, gathered them together, started them upon their errand of lawlessness and crime. You will remember that when they arrived at Wardner, as shown by the testimony of some three or four witnesses, that the order was, "Wardner to the front and Burke next." Now, whose agency was that from Burke that was being ordered to the second place in the battalion upon the 29th of April? Who had set in motion the physical power that was moving under that command? Even if the defendant was not there, still, as in the Spies case, where two of the men remained away and were not within hearing or within firing distance of the scene of the crime, yet they had helped to organize, had met with the men upon the Monday night before, had been with them, encouraged them, advised them and told them what to do; so, in this case upon the morning of the 29th, he had advised, encouraged and started them upon the expedition. In that case, the Monday night before was the last time that the two men that were afterwards hung were

with their co-spirators; but, in this case, we find that only
two hours before this killing, or four hours at the outside,
this defendant was in direct touch with the parties who
were ordered to the second place under the command on
the 29th of April, when the crime was committed.

Now, if we do that, if the evidence shows that at the time
the defendant met with his men upon the morning of the
29th and was discussing and planning this expedition, ad-
vising and encouraging it, that he had full knowledge of
its object and purposes, that is sufficient under the law to
warrant you in finding a verdict of guilty.

We have shown that the defendant was at Wardner just
prior to this trouble. Where do we next find Mr. Corcoran?
Upon the morning of the 29th, after the men had gathered
at the hall, Mr. Culbertson, the manager of the Tiger-Poor-
man mine, learns that none of his men had gone to work
upon that morning. Mr. Culbertson had lived in Burke for
a long time and was familiar with the situation. When his
men were not at their places, who did he send for, to whom
did he go to learn the cause? He was in touch with the
union, dealing with it from day to day, he knew the man
who had authority to speak, he knew who would know the
cause of their quitting and what they were going to do and
what the difficulty was and he naturally sent for the man
who could best advise him what the meeting at the union
hall signified. There is no stronger, more potent and
powerful proof of the influence of Mr. Corcoran over
that union than the fact that this manager, who dealt with
the union from day to day, operating his mine with union
men, instantly sent for him and him alone to find out what
was going on and why the men had quit work and when
they would return to their work again. When the manager
finds the defendant, what happens? When he first sent
in the hall for him, he could not get him—too busy preparing for the direful work of the day, too busy about
the preparation for arson and murder. But Culbertson
was not satisfied to consult any one else—if he consulted
any one else, they had no authority to speak and would not
speak—so he went again for this defendant—the general
in charge—and finding him at last, asked the defendant
about the cause of the difficulty, asked him, you remember,
if there was going to be trouble at Burke. In answer, the
defendant discloses his full knowledge of the situation, for
he says, "There is going to be no trouble in the canyon.

We are going to Wardner today." Yes, we are going to
Wardner, in full charge and in full possession of the destination and objects to be accomplished. The force he set in
motion there at Burke was the force which took the life
of James Cheyne.

Now, Gentlemen of the Jury, look back for a moment,
over the ground we have covered and see the facts mar-
shalled around this defendant. Remember, if you please,
that he is a member of the Cental Union, remember that
he is financial secretary, remember that just a few days
before the crime, he was seen consorting with the fomen-
tors of this trouble at Wardner, acquainting himself, undoubtedly, with the situation, remember that upon the
morning of the 29th at the hour when the men were gathering, and girding up their loins for the commission of crime,
this defendant told Culbertson precisely what they were
going to do and that the men would be back to go to work
on the night shift—all of which proved to be correct. Remember, above all, that within the wake of that mob, whose
course was so certainly foretold by the defendant, when
night came, lay the body of James Cheyne, from which life
was slowly ebbing. They have charged me, in this case,
with being remorseless—I court the charge, this supposed
contumely I prize most highly. I would that I could be as
remorseless for justice as the man who planned this hellish
expedition was remorseless for crime. Not crime mellowed
by the heat of passion, not crime which springs instantaneously from some lover's jealous heart, but cold, deliberate,
premeditated crime—the taking of the life of an innocent,
hard working, peaceable citizen, because, forsooth, he was,
as his slayers said, a "scab." I ask, in all candor and in
all sincerity, is there sufficient strength in the law, sufficient manhood in our jurors to protect the life of the
peaceful and industrous citizen! Answer me with your
verdict!

Now, who was the defendant speaking for when he re-
sponded to Culbertson? For his men who, when order was
given "Wardner to the front," and "Burke second," took
their place in the march to the mill and to the point where
they killed Cheyne. Did the defendant have knowledge of
what they were going there for, do you think that he was
mixing with the men that morning, with ears closed and
eyes shut, did this member of the Central Union, this secretary and leader have knowledge of the situation or did

he not? There is no denial of the Culbertson conversation, no denial of any of these incriminating facts, they are left to stand unchallenged and undisputed, and this being true, they are themselves sufficient to connect the defendant with this conspiracy, they show that he was a member of the conspiracy, a participant in this crime. So, let me say again, it seems that after his having told Mr. Culbertson, "We are going to Wardner," the defense ought to have disclosed when it was that the defendant changed his mind and withdrew from the conspiracy. He certainly intended to go when he spoke thus to Culbertson. Now, when was it he changed his mind—still the defense is silent and silence is all but a confession of crime.

Court adjourns for the dinner hour.

If Your Honor please and Gentlemen of the Jury, at the recess hour, I was discussing with you the events of the morning of the 29th. Particularly, with reference to the conversation between Mr. Culbertson and the defendant, showing defendant's connection with and knowledge of the conspiracy.

I desire to call your attention to a line of argument adduced by counsel for the defendant as to this point. He seemed to concede that we fully connect the defendant with this movement at Burke upon the morning of the 29th, but insisted before the jury, that there was no evidence of any criminal purpose at that time, upon the part of the mob; that notwithstanding the defendant might have been there, notwithstanding he associated and met with the men upon that morning, that all this could be true and still Mr. Corcoran have no knowledge of any criminal or unlawful purpose. He claims that the criminal and unlawful purpose was first evidenced after they got to the town of Gem.

Let me first direct your attention to the body of men who passed immediately from the union hall to the train as indicating the knowledge which they had of the criminal purpose of this movement. You will recall, gentlemen, that Burke was where they first took possession of the train. They did not go upon the train, as counsel would apparently have you believe, as men do who are going upon a peaceful errand, but they literally took possession of the train. Some hundred and fifty went upon the train and then sent two or three parties with Winchesters and revolvers to give the engineer instructions and these instructions the engineer received while covered with a Winches-

ter. This, you will recall, took place at the home town of
the defendant, within a few feet of the union hall and within
a few minutes of the time that we have proven Mr. Corcoran
to have been in the company of the very men who took posses
sion of the train. As I have said to you before, this fact
that these men had their arms, in possession of a magazine
of deadly weapons and the fact that they immediately,
after gathering and while still in the town of Burke, began
to exercise their power and then and there committed
breaches of the peace, discloses beyond a question, the fact
that the criminal purpose was already in their minds and
this while they were under the immediate control of the defendant. Just as those at Mullen marched down to the
rendezvous and dug up their secreted arms, just as those at
Gem went into the darkened hall and found their arms and
masks, so did those at Burke shoulder arms and take possession of the train. All showing plan, organization,
secrecy, criminal design. It is for you to say, after taking
into consideration all these facts and circumstances, the
situation, position and environments of the defendant,
whether the defendant and his associates, while they were
yet in Burke, had in mind, had knowledge of, the unlawfulness of the errand upon which they were bent. They
were then and there committing unlawful acts, controlling
the train and its crew by means of force and violence, and
we say, all this shows most conclusively that these men at
Mullen, Gem, Wardner and Burke knew that this day's
work should be done, not as suggested by the softly
fondled phrase of counsel, by means of "moral suasion"—
the hypocritical cant which they would use to shield murder—but by revolvers, Winchesters and dynamite.

But there is another significant fact, however much
counsel for defense may make light of it. Just as the train
was pulling out or about ready to go, a physician—at least
he denominates himself such and was passing as such in
the town of Burke, does yet, I believe—was passing the
train or near by. Mind you, these men were then upon the
train, in charge of it, with revolvers in their hands, directing the conductor and engineer, and also evidently looking
forward for serious trouble for they called upon this physician to go with them. What did they say to him, why did
they call him? Certainly, as you saw him upon the witness stand, diminutive, sickly, sorry, misbegotten—not for
his physical force, not certainly for his moral force in

this test of "moral suasion," for in that emaciated and
stunted form, was, as appears from his acts, a soul more
starved and stunted still, since he comes before you a cowardly, cringing, begging, self-confessed purjerer, wearing
in his form and in his moral figure, Nature's own brand
of disapproval. They called him because, as they said, they
thought they would have need of a physician. It is certain,
positively certain, that the mob fully contemplated and
understood from the beginning the unlawfulness of their
expedition, for they not only went armed and masked, not
only took forcible possession of the train, but also took
their physician with his surgical instruments, the same
physician who hurried to the side of Smith, the union man
who was killed, just as this physician was ordered to do
while on the train, going down from Burke. You will remember the physician testified that some masked man,
while they were on the train, told him that if there was any
firing, he should move to the point of the firing. Like Na-
poleon, he was to move to the point where the fighting was
fiercest.

This indicates more strongly than anything else could
the deadly, hellish, criminal purpose of the trip and that
the purpose was well understood from the start. They
knew force and violence were to be used, fighting was expected, crimes were to be committed. So, we find not only
was Mr. Corcoran there in the midst of the crowd, but in
the midst of the crowd which was armed and carrying
masks, the crowd which took possession by force of the
train, the crowd which took along the physician in case of
injuries occurring in the battle anticipated at the mill.
Now, do you think these subordinates knew of these things,
had knowledge of all these things and that the superior officer did not? Is that the logic of these facts?

I called your attention, before adjournment, to the fact
that a few days before, this defendant visited Wardner, the
seat of trouble. I called your attention to this because conditions were such at the time of his visit that he could not
have made the visit and remained ignorant of this growing
conspiracy, its object and purposes. But what do we find
in a few days after the riot? Shortly after the difficulty of
the 29th, we find that the defendant is introduced to Manager Joe McDonald, and for what purpose? What was the
occasion of this meeting with McDonald? To again act
as leader, to take control and look after the interests of the
union. He was there as a member of the Central Union to

try to arrange affairs between the unions and the Bunker Hill and Sullivan Company. How can it be reasoned that a man, who just before and just after and at the very time almost of the commission of the crime was in close touch with those who committed the crime, associating with them as their paid officer, how can it be reasoned for a moment even if there was no other evidence, that he could be innocent of what was going on and what was going to be done, especially when these facts are undisputed and uncontradicted facts? For, I repeat again, up to this time, the defense has not seen fit to dispute the fact that he was there with the men in the morning or his conversation with Culbertson or his being at Wardner or his meeting with Joe McDonald. Am I not justified? May not I fairly say to you that the legitimate inference from all these facts is that, if they had undertaken to dispute them, it would have opened a Pandora's box which they did not care to have you look into? Had they ever placed upon the stand a prominent officer of those unions, it is likely that upon cross-examination we would have unmasked the most revolting, the most infamous conspiracy ever nurtured in these canyons.

But there is another witness who adds much to the question of Mr. Corcoran's relation to the events of that morning. That is the witness, Mr. Stringham. He is a resident of Burke. So far as the evidence discloses, he is not an employee of the Bunker Hill and Sullivan Mining Company and is not, therefore, subject to the stereotyped attack of counsel for the defense. As I say, he has resided in Burke for years, engaged in business. His standing for truth has not been assailed, he comes before you a disinterested citizen who saw what he saw while going about his business that morning. What does he say? He says that upon the morning of the 29th, he saw Mr. Corcoran going up the street with a gun in his hands or upon his shoulder —I disremember which, but the gun was in his possession. But counsel for the defense say this witness testified that he took it for a gun. The very fact that Mr. Stringham does not come here and with immaculate certainty say that he knows it was a gun is all the more reason, it seems to me, that his testimony should commend itself to you. He stated that he saw Mr. Corcoran, of that he was positive and stated to you that he had in his possession that which he took to be a gun—he did not personally examine it—but there was no doubt, in his mind, but what it was a gun, as there is none in yours. Mr. Stringham is a neighbor of Mr. Corcoran and comes here reluctantly enough—he was anything but a free and willing witness and tells what he knows. They permit his testimony to stand undenied and his character unattacked. I ask you, as fair men, what will you do with such testimony? Will you discard it or will you believe it? If his testimony be true, then we not only find that the defendant was there acting with the mob, but we find him with arms, going to join his comrades who were also arming and masking for the horrible work of the day. And a few minutes after he is seen with a gun, they seize the train and move down to the place where they took the life of James Cheyne.

But we not only have the testimony of Mr. Stringham upon this point, but we have the testimony of a gentleman whom Mr. Robertson styles, with his peculiar hyperboles, "a kid-glove cess-pool." My friend Robertson seems to have all the metaphorical madness of a poet, though, perhaps, his figures of speech are not quite as classical nor quite as apt as the best style of literature would demand. And here let me say in regard to this witness that this is another instance in which they have fallen down in their promises of proof. They say that he is a notorious liar, that he is a horse thief from the State of Montana and they have promised you that they would bring the records to prove that fact, but no records are here. They also told you that they would bring Mr. Malvey to disprove St. Clair's statement, and, although Mr. Malvey is one of their fast friends, he has not the courage to take the witness stand. So, we have Mr. St. Clair, unattacked, save by the words of counsel, testifying that Mr. Corcoran was the man who called the union meeting upon that morning and testifying that Mr. Malvey also told him that Mr. Corcoran was the man who called the meeting. So, we have Mr. Culbertson and Mr. Stringham and Mr. St. Clair, uncontradicted and unimpeached, testifying to this state of facts which show, beyond question, that Mr. Corcoran was there organizing the mob upon the morning of the 29th. Now, I ask you, was the defendant a member of this conspiracy? Was he cognizant of what was going on? Did he know what was to be done upon that day? Was he oblivious of the fury and madness, the criminal purpose of that mob? Was he deaf to their shouts of defiance to law and their threats of crime? Was he blind to the sight of masks and Winchesters?

But, Gentlemen of the Jury, let's follow him closer still to the scene of the killing and bind him closer to his crime. We shall not stop with the defendant's acts of the morning of the 29th at Burke. We insist that the evidence shows conclusively that he was present and participated in the killing. A great deal has been said about the fact that we have called, as witnesses, many who have been in the employ of the Bunker Hill and Sullivan Mining Company. I am now going to ask you to listen to the testimony of a man who was never in their employ but is an associate and the fellow-official of this defendant. A man who undoubtedly knew the defendant just as well as I know His Honor upon the bench; associating with him for years as a fellow-workman, part of the time in the same mine; a fellow-official in the same lodge; a man whose every interest and whose every purpose would naturally be to conceal anything that might identify Mr. Corcoran or connect him with this crime. Certainly there can be no reason to charge, if there has been a warping of testimony in this case upon the part of Mr. Clark, that it has been through the influence of the State. At the time that Mr. Clark testified in this case, at the time that he gave this testimony upon which we rely, Mr. Corcoran was not under arrest and my associates and myself had, up to that time, nothing to do with the prosecution. We, whom they say are paid by the Bunker Hill and Sullivan Mining Company for the purpose of hanging an innocent man, had no more to do with the prosecution at that time than had one of you. It was long prior to our appearance in the case and at a time when the reason for an alibi upon the part of the defense had not arisen. At a time when the alibi had not become a necessary factor in the case. Mr. Clark states as positively as a man could state it in the English language, that he saw Mr. Corcoran within a short distance of the place of the killing and within a short time after the killing had taken place.

In all fairness, let us take into consideration the time, the conditions, the circumstances and the influences which were evidently controlling the mind of Mr. Clark at the time he gave this testimony before the coroner's jury. I want to read just a few words of this testimony in order to comment upon it intelligently. This is the testimony which Mr. Clark gave before the coroner's jury, which is testified to by him in this case as being the testimony which he gave before the coroner's jury: "I did not see Paul going down on the road." Notice the familiarity with which he speaks of this man as to whom they say he might have been mistaken. "I did not see Paul"—a fellow-official, a fellow-lodgeman— "on the road going down." Another thing I desire to direct your attention to is the fact that this information is volunteered upon the part of Clark. When I say volunteered, I will explain to you what I mean by the next sentence: "Did you see him after you got there? A. I did not see him in Wardner. I saw him on the train going back. Q. On the train going back? A. Yes. Q. Where? A. He was sitting on the top of a box car when I saw him."

Do you believe that at this time some master hand, as insinuated by counsel, was moulding the testimony of Mr. Clark? Do you believe that, with the powers of omniscience, some attorney foresaw the exact position upon the car and upon the train, that it would be necessary to have him in order to suit the position to the testimony of the Colborns. This is a wonderfully strong circumstance that Mr. Clark, away back before the coroner's jury, places this man in exactly the same position that all these other witnesses testify they found him in farther up the road. When you consider the time when this testimony was given and that Mr. Clark was a friend and fellow secretary of the defendant, and consider not only the fact that he saw him upon that day, but the place upon the car where he places him in this wonderfully "dangerous position," these are almost invincible facts. But let us read farther: "Q. Before you got to Burke? A. Yes, sir; between Wardner and Wallace. Q. How long have you known Paul Corcoran? A. About three years. Q. You know him intimately, do you? A. Well, yes; I may say I do. I know him any time I see him Q. That is, you could not be mistaken in the man?" Notice the significance of his answer, "Well, hardly." As if I should see one of my associates at this bar with whom I have been associated for years and some one should ask, "Could you be mistaken in Mr. Hawley, or Mr. Forney, or would you be deceived in the manly form of my friend, Robertson?" Why it would be—

Mr. ROBERTSON: ' I object to the testimony on the ground
that it is not in evidence.

THE COURT: Yes, that evidence was admitted, Mr. Robertson.

MR. BORAH: This is a transcript from the notes taken
in this court.

MR. ROBERTSON: I take an exception.

MR. BORAH: Allow me to say to you, Gentlemen of the
Jury—because I certainly would not stand here before you
and read testimony that had never been given—that this
is the testimony which was transcribed from the notes
taken in this case as the testimony which Mr. Clark said
he gave at the coroner's inquest. He stated to you himself
that this is the exact testimony as he gave it there before
the coroner: "Q. How long have you known Mr. Corcoran? A. About three years. Q. You know him intimately? A. I know him any time I see him. Q. You could
not be mistaken in the man? A. Hardly. Q. Where
abouts on the train did you see him that day? A. Sitting on
top of a box car, going to get in a box car. Q. He was
sitting on it? A. Yes, sir. Q. You were not mistaken in
the man, were you? A. No. Q. He was sitting on the end
of the car? A. No, on the side."

Notice the peculiarity, the exact position he gives this
man upon that car. Does the interrogator ask him, "Was
he sitting in the middle of the car? Or even suggest it to
him? He asks where he was sitting and whether or not on
the end of the car, but Mr. Clark states that he was sitting
upon the side of the car when he reached home that afternoon and jumped off the car.

Gentlemen of the Jury, that evidence itself and alone
ought to be sufficient to satisfy a man that this man was
upon that train. Why should you, as men, doubt that evidence given under the circumstances under which it was?
Why should you say that this man, at a time when Mr.
Corcoran was not upon trial, not even arrested for the
crime, at a time when he had no reason to build up any defense of alibi and at a time when the witness was his fellow-official and his friend, give testimony which is in direct
corroboration, even to the minutiæ, with the evidence
which the State has produced here before you? He is not
subject to the criticism which they have made with reference to other witnesses whom, they claim, are interested.
He is interested again us as I shall show you in a few

moments. "You are positive you saw him sitting on that box car?"

MR. ROBERTSON: I again object to the testimony on the ground that it is not the testimony before the coroner's inquest and I refer to the testimony of the stenographer that is over here.

THE COURT: One objection is sufficient. (Exception.)

MR. BORAH, continuing: "You are positive you saw him sitting on that box car? A. Yes, sir. Q. That was between here and Wallace? A. It was the first stop we made out of Wardner here, and the train slowed up for some cause or other and I got out of the box car to get into another one, and, as I passed by, I seen Paul. Q. Did you see him prior to the time in the morning? A. I did not. Oh, I did see him at Burke in the morning." Now, there is the testimony, Gentlemen of the Jury, not of the Bunker Hill and Sullivan Mining Company, not of St. Clair, not of the mine owners of this region, not of the interested witnesses of the State, as they call them, but the fellow-secretary, the follow-lodgeman, the long years a Miners' Union man—John Clark.

What will you do with that testimony? Would you prefer to believe that Mr. Clark was mistaken when he said he saw this man with whom he had been associated for years or that perhaps Mac Malvey was mistaken as to the exact hour of the time when he saw him in the morning? Which is the more probable? If you should meet your neighbor, you would certainly know whether or not it was your neighbor. Especially if you had been associating with him for years in a close capacity; but there is nothing so difficult as to fix the hour when you saw a party upon a particular day when you are seeing him every day. But here was an extraordinary occasion; an extraordinary expedition. Mr. Clark had seen him that morning in the town of Burke; knew his dress; knew his make-up; knew his insignia of identification. Some three or four hours afterwards he saw him sitting on the top of a box car. Do you think he was mistaken or is it more reasonable to suppose that Miss Murphy and some of the other alibi witnesses were mistaken as to the exact hour of the day in which they saw him upon that day. It seems to me that when you come to weigh the testimony of Mr. Clark, and the circumstances that surrounded the giving of it, and the relation of Mr. Clark to this man, that you must be satisfied that

Mr. Corcoran was upon the train coming up from Wardner to Wallace upon that day. If he was there, he was there for an unlawful purpose. If he was there, he was there for the same reason that the other men were there. If he was there, he was there branded with the same idea of crime as every other man that went upon that expedition.

It is true, Gentlemen of the Jury, that Mr. Clark has stated before you—and I want to refer to that briefly—that at this present time he has reason to doubt the correctness of his testimony before the coroner's jury. I shall refer to this in connection with another matter, but I want to briefly refer to it at this time. He states to you that owing to the fact that he has had many conversations with "the boys" (to use his own language), that he is inclined to doubt that he knew this man Corcoran with whom he had been associating so long, his fellow-official. But imagine the influence which must have been brought to bear upon him at the time that that doubt was created in his mind. If you were well acquainted with a man, had been associating with him for years and were a fellow-official, what kind of influence would it take to make you doubt that proposition? I apprehend that it was not the influence of this so-called corruption fund that counsel talk so much about. The influence was not wrought in that direction. It was another influence, a more potent and powerful influence, and one which the State has had to contend with in this case from its inception. The influence which has made brave men cowards in this community for seven years.

After we leave Mr. Clark, we take up the testimony of Mrs. Sinclair. She testifies that upon the morning of the 29th, she was in the vicinity of the killing and at the time of the shooting of Mr. Cheyne, she went immediately to the scene and was there at the time Cheyne was shot. There is no dispute about her being there; there is no dispute but that, woman-like, she risked her own life as she sprang to 'the help of this wounded man. There is no dispute but that she walked down the road with Cheyne after he was picked up and was being led away; that she was there and had an opportunity to see, their own witnesses admit. She testifies that when she plead for some one to come and help her take care of Cheyne, she saw the defendant standing in the midst of the posse from whence the shot was fired that killed Cheyne. She says that she had an opportunity to

view him, to see his eyes, his mustache and his general
figure, the peculiar droop of his shoulders. She had seen
him a couple of weeks before and she saw him here upon the
witness stand. She looked directly at the defendant when
asked the question and stated to this jury that that was
the same man she saw there on the 29th of April. You
should consider her testimony also in connection with
Clark's and Culbertson's and Stringham's and St. Clair's,
who saw him going to and from the place where Mrs. Sinclair says she saw him standing at the time the fatal shot
was fired. They claim, however, that the fact that the defendant was masked would disidentify him to such an ex-
tent that it would make her testimony unreliable. Of
course, that mask was put on for that purpose—of en-
abling them to prove more successfully an alibi. The effect
which they claim for it now is the exact effect which was
hoped for when the mask was put on. But this is not the
first time that men have gone upon an expedition of crime
thinking they are securely concealed and yet have been detected. The labyrinth of crime is always dark and conceal-
ment is always coveted, but through some weak part of the
shield, fate puts its finger and lets in the light. Many a
man has hid himself behind the curtains of the night and
thought himself secure, to learn in after hours that the eye
of retributive justice was at all times full upon him. In
this particular instance, it was the quick, sure eye of a
brave and pleading woman which unerringly detected the
cowardly assassin lurking behind the hideous mask. An
angel of mercy, stooping to uplift the victim, turns fully
upon the skulking form of the murderer and marks him for
his fate. She saw that same cold eye you have doubtless
observed here often, she saw the same figure, heard the
same voice, noticed the same drooping shoulders and
marked well in that instance all his features—it was Paul
Corcoran standing there with those who killed James
Cheyne—one of them.

But Colonel Reddy says her testimony is evidently false.
Colonel Reddy has been engaged in the practice of criminal
law for years. He has spent the best part of his busy life in
clearing men charged with crime. But I will venture the
assertion that never in his life has he known a woman to
wilfully testify falsely for the purpose of convicting a man.
It is not in accord with woman's nature, with her sympathetic, impulsive, kindly being. It is once in ten thousand

times when they do such a thing. You may work upon her sympathies, upon her responsive nature, upon her friend-ship, upon her family associations and in behalf of distress make her believe that is true which is not true, but seldom for the purpose of inflicting punishment or visiting distress upon others. Some may go farther, perhaps, and under such circumstances knowingly warp their testimony, in be-half of a friend, but seldom, indeed, in the annals of crime, has it been found that a woman testified falsely for the pur-pose of hanging a man. Measure the superlative womanhood of this witness. See her actions upon that day, her cool-ness, her bravery, the intrepidity with which she walked to the side of the prostrate Cheyne, from whom men were fleeing—at a time when, as their own witnesses tell you, bullets were pattering around her like hail—matchless, in-describable womanhood, grandest in the surprised ordeals of life. See these things and tell me, if you can, that she lied in order to send this defendant to the scaffold.

But I must hasten on as I am consuming more time than I had anticipated I would. We next notice the testimony of Mr. and Mrs. Colborn, which corroborates the testimony of Mr. Clark. These parties saw the defendant as he was passing their house, identified him positively, saw him upon the same place upon the car that Clark did. The de-fendant was their landlord, had been for some time. They were well acquainted with him.

The defense introduced some photographs here for the purpose, I presume, of showing that the train ran by so quickly that the human eye could not measure the distance so instantaneously and be able to note the person that was passing. I assume that the photographs were introduced for that purpose, although they seem to be a little mysteri-ous as to their reasons for introducing these photographs. But the defense did not see fit to experiment upon this proposition. They did not see fit to disclose by experiment that this could not be done, but in view of the fact that they were apparently urging this so strongly, the prosecution took it up and demonstrated, by actual experiment, that a person could be easily seen passing upon the car from the point where the Colborns stood. They have been much amused, apparently, about the fact that we took a pic-turesque ride the other morning in order to demonstrate this fact, but, nevertheless, it demonstrated it very thor-oughly. We placed witnesses at the point where the Colborns stood and ran the train by at full speed with parties upon the box cars and all of the parties passing were easily identified. There seemed to be no difficulty in either identifying the parties or in riding upon the box cars.

We have another witness who saw him get off the train at Burke going home that night. They were claiming that the manner in which he jumped off the train was impossible, but we demonstrated that fact also by actual experiments. We showed that it was an easy matter to ride on the box car and a perfectly safe thing to jump off the box car as it has been testified Mr. Corcoran did when he arrived at Burke upon the evening of the 29th.

Now, Gentlemen of the Jury, we have returned to the city of Burke. We started in the morning with the preparation upon the part of Mr. Corcoran, as testified to by Mr. Culbertson, and we have followed him through the testimony of Mr. Clark, Mrs. Sinclair, Mr. St. Clair, Stringham, Mr. and Mrs. Colborn, upon this entire expedition. When you take these facts and place them upon the background of his position, his relation to these institutions or these organizations, take into consideration the fact that he was the financial secretary, that he was a member of the Central Union, that he was a paid officer of this organization, there can be no reasonable doubt of the fact that he was also a member of this conspiracy and actually participating from its beginning to the close. And, as I have said to you before, if he was a member of the conspiracy, that is sufficient under the law whether he actually fired the shot which killed James Cheyne or not.

THE DEFENSE—ALIBI.

What is their defense in this case, Gentlemen of the Jury? What answer have they given to all this proof and to these charges? What showing has he made to the proof that we have introduced that he was a member of the conspiracy? Do they introduce any evidence that he was not a part and parcel of the conspiracy? We contend not, for the simple reason that all their evidence simply goes to show that he remained at Burke while the mob went down to Wardner, and yet he might have remained at Burke and been a most active member of the conspiracy. They have introduced no official of the union; they have brought forward no evidence to disconnect the union with these acts upon the 29th. They have left the testimony of Culbertson and Stringham and St. Clair and Mrs. Sinclair and Clark entirely undisputed. They do not contend, through the lips of witnesses that the defendant was not a member of the conspiracy; they simply contend that as a matter of argument. The fact that he might have remained in Burke, as I have said, could be true and yet he be a member of the conspiracy. The fact that he was at Burke at 12 o'clock might be true and yet he might be a most powerful agent in the taking of the life of James Cheyne. He might do as Spies and Nichol did, he might remain away while his agents and associates went forth to commit the crime. Have they met this question? Have they presented anything for you to consider upon this proposition? They have practically left the matter without contradiction and yet the counsel for the defense tel's you that the State evidently does not expect a conviction. I will tell you what I do expect. I expect that when such evidence is brought before honest jurymen, upright men and it is permitted to go undenied, that that evidence will be sufficient to satisfy your consciences.

They find much fault because my associate, in opening this argument, stated that it was evident that the town of Burke was in sympathy with the defense and that for that reason you should scrutinize the testimony very carefully of all those alibi witnesses who come from Burke. I shall not, for want of time, be able to go into detail with reference to the testimony of those witnesses, but allow me to call your attention to a few facts which justify, as it seems to me, in every respect, the statement of my associate, Mr. Hawley. I do not ask you to discard entirely, as Mr. Robertson says, and without examination, the testimony of all these witnesses nor do I ask you to refrain from making a close analysis of their testimony with a view of finding out whether or no it be true, but I want you to look into the environments and circumstances which surround those witnesses, together with a few facts with reference to some individual witnesses.

You all know, from experience, that when you find witnesses whose sympathies are thoroughly aroused in favor of the party upon trial, they are very easily influenced. I undertake to say that it might be true that the greater portion of these women who have testified in this case actually believe that they saw Mr. Corcoran upon that day and yet be entirely mistaken. I will tell you why. In the first place, you have noticed that Mr. John Clark, a man of mature years, a man not only of positive convictions and with much individuality, but a man of much experience, testified that he saw this defendant at Wardner upon the 29th and afterwards stated that, owing to conversations with friends of the defendant, he had come to doubt his own word and his own eye-sight. As I said to you, imagine the powerful influence which must have been brought to bear upon Mr. Clark to cause him to doubt the fact that he saw a man with whom he had been associated for years. Then place that influence, that moulding, controlling, powerful influence around a sympathetic girl like Maggie Murphy and see what it will do, or Mrs. Smith or Mrs. Walker, whose sympathies, they say, are thoroughly aroused in favor of Mr. Corcoran. Counsel say that it is a terrible charge to insinuate that this influence has been exercised. I simpl reply that Mr. Clark himself revealed this influence and that it is proper and legitimate for me to reason that the influence, which caused Mr. Clark to doubt his own words, might make much difference with the testimony of a 16-year-old girl—might make her honestly believe that she saw the defendant at 11 o'clock instead of 10 o'clock. He was in the town of Burke at 10 o'clock; he was back there at 6 o'clock. He was only out of town a few hours and nothing is more difficult to place the exact hour in which you see a man when you see him every day.

Counsel for the defense exultingly exclaim that I was first to discover Miss Murphy. That they did not know of her as a witness until I went to Burke and had a conversation with her. I am very proud of this discovery. She was certainly the most admirably appearing witness upon the stand for the defense. I did discover Miss Murphy in a sense, I guess, but I don't flatter myself that I discovered her before Mr. Robertson did. But you noticed the little Miss Murphy as she sat beside Mrs. Corcoran here in the court room; she is evidently on close terms with the family, apparently part and parcel of the family, and, as she was frank to state, all her feelings and sympathies were aroused in their favor. There is nothing more easy than to make a party believe that 10 o'clock is 11 o'clock when you have to recall the matter over two months past. Miss Murphy says that there is nothing by which she can fix the time in her mind, except that she was setting the table; says it might have been 10 o'clock or it might have been 11 o'clock, and if it was 10 o'clock, then he could have been there and gone on the train also. Her sister was upon the stand also, but she states to you, upon cross-examination, that she does not know whether it was before or after the train went out that day. So, I say to you, that it is not necessary for you, as jurymen, to come to the conclusion that this young girl wilfully testified to a falsehood, but it does seem, from all the facts and circumstances, that she must have been mistaken as to the hour.

But another fact with reference to this question of outside influence. You will remember that Dr. Collins, poor, pitiable, self-confessed purgerer, testified before you that, in the inception of this investigation before the coroner's jury, he had sworn to a falsehood. Why did he do so? Was it by reason of this "corruption fund," this bugaboo which forced my friend Robertson into an ecstacy of frenzy? Was it by reason of the fact that Mr. Campbell has grown rich, as Mr. Robertson says, in a few years? No, it was by reason, as Dr. Collins says of the influence of these men who wore masks and carried arms on the 29th day of April. This subtle, intangible force which cannot be described, measured or known to any man until he comes in contact with it—this influence which has paralyzed many a man with fear who was a braver man than Dr. Collins. Now, what effect do you think such influence would have upon a man like Mr. Kelly, who was a member of this same organization? This is the power which has moulded the testimony of these witnesses; this is the power that influenced Mr. Clark and which has controlled them all more or less. Was not my associate justified when he stated to you that these witnesses came from a place where this influence was most intense? There is another thing that shows, beyond a question, that these witnesses have been wrought upon in this manner. They could not tell when they saw Mr. Corcoran upon any other day or at any other time. They could remember that they saw him ordinarily from day to day, but as to the place, the time, the particular day, the week or month, they could tell us nothing except upon the day of the 29th, and then they could give the hour and the minute. This day lives so vividly in their memory that it has effaced every thing else. Let's look at this in the most charitable way. Why is it that these witnesses could remember the 29th with certainty even to the minute, some of them stating fifteen minutes to

11 o'clock, some of them thirty minutes after 11 o'clock, fixing not only the hour, but the minute and without any memorandum and yet could not tell this jury of another instance when they saw the defendant. You know that one of two things is true—either that they have been made to believe that they saw him and honestly think so or that they have permitted themselves to be used to rescue their friend. I am willing for you to take the more charitable view of the matter.

They put a man by the name of Brass upon the witness stand. I think the gentleman has been properly named. He was a man of mature years and certainly calculated to remember as well as any one else. But I want to call your attention to his testimony. He testified that upon the 29th, at noon or thereabouts, Mr. Corcoran came to purchase some meat, made a purchase at his store. Now, he said he had no way on earth to fix that time except from general recollection, about 12 o'clock, he said, or thereabouts. We called for his books in this instance and what do we find? It was strange that they did not call for this book, but they did not do so. If this book is a memorandum of the business of that man, as he says, it ought to be better than any memory. They did not call for the book. They put him upon the witness stand and with the same ease and the same comfort as the other witnesses, he testified that he saw Corcoran about 12 o'clock and he would have gone off the witness stand unshaken had we not called for the book ourselves. We find, from examination of the book, that the entry for this purchase is upon the 30th of April. Now, Gentlemen of the Jury, just notice how very easy it is for this man to change his testimony so as to fit the defense of alibi. He had the transaction with Mr. Corcoran, the purchase of the meat and it took place about 12 o'clock, but it was upon the 30th and so he just changed the day and his story was as complete and brief as a summer serial. But again, here are ten or fifteen entries in the book in the same hand writing, made upon the same day to parties living in the town of Burke and yet Mr. Brass could not tell you the name of a single one and fix the hour when he made the purchase. Now, I ask you in all candor and in all fairness, how do you suppose that Brass fixed Mr. Corcoran's time for 12 o'clock, April 29th? Gentlemen of the Jury, I am not willing that, so far as Mr. Brass is concerned, that he

should be considered in the list of those whom you should
look upon in a charitable way. This book, in his own hand
writing, proves that he has deliberately testified falsely.
So they call another witness to the same effect, Mr.
Baumgartner. He testifies that he saw him at 3 o'clock. I
ask him how he knows that it was 3 o'clock and he says,
"I guess I know the time of day." I ask him how he fixed
the time. He says, "I guess I can fix the time." And so
we go on for five or ten minutes asking him in all fairness
to give this jury the means by which he fixes that time and
the only thing that you can get from him is, "I guess I come
pretty near knowing the time of day." But he disclosed his
unfairness of disposition and his desire to conceal something in another way. I ask him if he was in sympathy
with the union. Now, he knows whether he is or not, doesn't
he? What does he say to you? He said he did not know
whether he was or not. He was not satisfied in
his mind as to what effect that kind of testimony would have before the jury and therefore he withheld it. Now, there are some five or six of that class of witnesses who come before you and testify that they are members of the Miners' Union, and were in Burke
that day and saw the defendant. I do not say,
of course, that simply because they were members of the union that it would necessarily follow that they
would testify to a falsehood. There are just as good men
members of the union as there are anywhere else to be
found and lots of them, but I do say that when you take
into consideration that there was an effort upon the part
of the union that day to get every single member down to
Wardner for the purpose of destroying this property and
running out these men, and when you take into consideration that they were able to gather together one hundred and
fifty men who were willing to go forth and violate the law
and commit crime, it is not surprising that they can go gack
to that town of Burke and find six more who are willing to
protect the man who did commit the crime. Counsel for
the defense say that it is an extraordinary thing for us to
contend that these people are so saturated with feeling that
they will protect this defendant by manufactured testimony. True, it is an awful thing to say; but if I had told
you upon the 26th day of April or the 27th or the 28th, that
you could go into the town of Burke and get one hundred
and fifty men who would be willing to go forth and destroy

$250,000 worth of property and take human life, Mr. Robertson and Colonel Reddy would have arisen in their wrath and denounced it as a lie. Nevertheless, it was an easy thing to do. They gathered those men together on the morning of the 29th. One hundred and fifty from the little town of Burke, who were willing to band themselves—for the purpose of arson and indiscriminate murder, and yet they say that, because we charge that nine or ten more can be gathered together out of the same town for the purpose of protecting this man, we are reasoning without conscience before the jury. Do you believe that when men will go forth to commit these crimes, band themselves together for the purpose of violating law, that their associates, the men left behind, will hesitate to come forth for the purpose of protecting them when it is done? That is the reason why we say you should measure the testimony of these men with care. You should consider their testimony almost precisely the same as you would of a man who was actually in the conspiracy. When they come upon the witness stand and say that they are not only members of the union, but that they are in sympathy with the union in this present contest, you must look with care upon their testimony. Notice that the witnesses do not say, "I did sympathize with the union, but I do not approve of their conduct upon the 29th." They have not separated from the union. They are still sympathizers with it, and hence we feel justified in saying to you that you must look upon their testimony as you would any man's who was testifying under the pressure of passion and prejudice. If witnesses are willing to go upon the stand in sympathy with those who committed the crime, is it very far from that point to where they are willing to protect the man who committed the crimes?

Another thing, Gentlemen of the Jury, you will observe that, notwithstanding the city of Burke has a considerable population outside of some ten or fifteen whom they called, yet no clerk, no druggist, no merchant, no business man, no hotel keeper, no restaurant keeper, no one of that kind has been called here to testify that Mr. Corcoran was seen upon the streets that day. The witnesses who have been called here, six of them are members of the union, four wives of men who are members of the union, and some of them now in incarceration and two are relatives of this defendant. These are the people they have gathered together in the little town of Burke to testify in behalf of the defendant.

All these things are for you to consider and, as fair and candid men, try to arrive at a just conclusion as to the guilt or innocence of the defendant.

This is all the time that I can spend upon the testimony, but permit me, Gentlemen of the Jury, before I close, to again disclaim, both personally and as a representative of the State, all intention of attacking organized labor as such. I want to leave the brand of contempt upon that malicious falsehood. It is as wilful as it is base, as despicable as it is unfair.

It is not only the right, but the imperative, duty of labor to organize. The men who endure the hardships, bear the burdens and incur the risks of underground mining, are certainly entitled to every advantage which lawful organization can give them. Labor organizations, upon a legitimate basis and for a legitimate purpose, are not only entitled to the respect but to the encouragement and protection of the public and the State. Organizations which would foster the manhood, nourish the Americanism and elevate the mind and character of its members are a grand thing. They bridle the greed, check the stately tread of capital, they unite the interests and harmonize the action and forces of labor, they protect the homes, brighten the hearthstones and gladden the face of wife and mother as she bends above her loved one in the ecstacy of a mother's infinite love, dreaming of its future years. I am in favor of them because I know, when properly conducted, they nourish the citizenship, encourage patriotism and more effectually enables the laborer to rear his family and place within their reach the torch of learning.

God knows these grand old institutions of ours, so long the asylum of the oppressed, must crumble and fall like the splendid, but false fabric of ancient days, unless the countless homes of American workmen of every class are shielded from the ignorance and poverty which blights manhood and destroys citizenship. Every organization, which has for its object these purposes, should receive the blessing of patriot and saint, for they are just and righteous altogether.

MURDER SOCIETY.

But I am speaking to you today of an organization which has been wrenched from its original purpose and turned into the channels of crime, which would convert the man who labors into a secret, masked and treacherous outlaw, separate him from his home, make him a fugitive from his State and a suspect in the bosom of his own family; an organization which uses the American flag as a mask to conceal the cowardly face of the lurking assassin and which strikes at the very foundation of our whole system of government by openly destroying property and taking human life; an organization which shrinks from the open light of day, which, in darkened rooms and secret hiding places away from the conscience-smiting power of even a vagrant ray, gives to its adherents to drink of the blood from the skull of the last victim and administers that manhood murdering oath which renders him who takes in an Ishmaelite of the social world, an outlaw with humanity, a stranger to the nobler and higher impulses of man's moral being.

"By the pricking of my thumbs,
Something wicked this way comes."

And the weird, wild and secret hags of anarchy hold high carnival over the fallen and forfeited manhood of the sturdy but misguided workman.

I say to you that the organization which hides from the open light of day, whose members flee before the dawn, "like a guilty thing upon a fearful summons," is not an organization which can represent the dignity, the manhood and patriotism of American labor or the Western miner.

What do you think of that organization which nourishes a spirit of hatred toward our institutions and contempt for the flag? Does it represent the sentiment of that class of men whose bravery made sacred every battlefield of the war for the Union and whose sterling heroism and sturdy loyalty have in so many instances added glory to the American arms in the late war? We have seen that, while the mob was congregated near the scene of its cowardly crimes of April 29th, they repeatedly cried out, "Down with America, Down with America." I almost wish that those who gave utterance to such sentiments, a sentiment which stirs to its last dregs all the hatred of my soul, could be scourged back to the old country and placed again under the bloody wheels of that old Juggernaut car of oppression until they would cry out in the agony of their dwarfed and stunted souls for the land which has been a common refuge for the laboring man for centuries. "Down with America." And that is the sentiment of the Western miner. I say it is a lie. I refuse to let counsel for the defense fasten upon them such an infamous stigma. It is the sentiment of anarchists and murderers who despise all forms of law and hate all forms of government.

CRIME'S MASQUERADE.

What we are fighting is crime, even though it masquerade under the garb of labor. What we say is that murder shall not go unpunished, though it parade in the guise of the honest miner. Men shall not transform labor organizations into combinations and conspiracies for assassination, and we believe you will say the same. If a man should burn your house above you, would you exonerate him because he was a member of a union? If he should burglarize your home or insult your family or steal your property or murder your son, would you say he is a member of a miner's union? No. You would say no combination shall work as a shield for the thief or the robber or he who takes life. He is a violator of law and shall be punished.

Let us look at this affair face to face as between man and man. Be honest with ourselves and faithful to the higher appeals of our better thoughts. What had poor Cheyne done? What offense had he committed? What wrong was he guilty of? He, too, was a laborer, earning his bread by daily toil, and life was as dear to him as you or I. He had oppressed no man, harmed no man, yet he was murdered, shot down like the game fleeing before the hunter, and in yonder city, in the cheerless gloom of the hospital, he yielded up his young life, a sacrifice to the wanton depravity of the most heartless of criminals. But when we ask that the slayers be punished, counsel, in their misguided zeal, cry out, "We are attacking labor." We ask for the punishment of a crime which has not a single softening feature to relieve it of its awful barbarity, and they reply, "You are attacking labor."

In the name of the 10,000 law-abiding miners scattered throughout this inter-mountain country, and in the name of labor everywhere, I deny this vicious libel, this base and senseless slander.

THE CRUCIAL TEST.

Gentlemen, yours is the most serious task of any who are connected with this important trial. You have been selected with much care, and to you are intrusted far more than the ordinary responsibilities of citizenship. The people of the state feel that the honor of the commonwealth, the very sovereignty of the State, are upon trial. And it is true. We are practically testing the efficiency and strength of our State government. Will it protect property? Is life secure within the dominion? Is law its supreme and guiding force? Does justice reign within its temples? What is this splendid fabric which the restless energy and indomitable courage of the old pioneer has carved from the wild waste of the great Northwest and set as a gem in the crown of our common country? Is it, in fact and in truth, a commonwealth where men can dwell together in peace and safety and women and children rest in the sacred security of the home, where industry may secure its just reward and enterprise have its merited protection? Can the law-abiding and industrius and peace-loving citizen find shelter beneath its sovereign power? Has it power to punish crime?

Or is it but a miserable pretense; a shameless, deluding mockery, where anarchy rules with ruthless sway, and the most revolting of crimes go unwhipped before the altar, where murder walks the streets of your town, selects its victim with indifference and slays him with impunity, yes, more, in the very presence of death the officers of the law laugh hyena-like above the prostrate victim and dance above the bleeding form like spirits incarnate from the crypts of hell.

These are questions you must answer, matters upon which you must pass. It is for you to say what our young state shall do. Shall high-handed crime continue within her midst and ply its trade in open defiance of law? Is our young State to become the rendezvous for criminals, the by-word of sister States? Is our State's pride forfeited? Is our manhood dead? I appeal to you, as men and citizens, give back the reign of law; deal fairly but fearlessly with those who would continually trample all authority and the State's honor beneath the feet of lawless vengeance.

To you I now submit the whole cause, and may the power which works for the betterment of all give unto you the righteousness of judgment which will enable you to deal in justice and without fear of man or the dread of man between this defendant and your sovereign State.

I thank you again and again for your attention and the exercise of your patience and submit this matter for its final adjudication in the court of your own conscience.

www.ingramcontent.com/pod-product-compliance
Lightning Source LLC
Chambersburg PA
CBHW021544270326
41930CB00008B/1358